A taste of
Holy Island - Lindisfarne
Northumberland and the Borders

Recipes by Victoria Mundy   Photographs and text by Roy Player

Stories from the Holy Island Archives   Edited by Jackie Hamley

isbn 978-1-904446-80-4

Acknowledgments

We have to say a huge thank you to the islands museum for their archives and in particular the articles by Elfreda Elford that were to be found in The Holy Island Times. Our thanks to Kyle Luke who is currently running the Crown and Anchor for the use of some wonderful archive photographs. To Heathershaw Mill for the historic images of the mill. To the PDSA for their wonderful work and allowing us to use the image of John and Sheila.

We have made every effort to ensure that any material that has not been generated by the authors, or friends of the authors, has been credited properly and, or, permission has been granted for the use of the material. If by any chance something has been used or credited incorrectly please do let us know and we shall address accordingly when we next print the book. And please accept our apologies if any offence has occurred.

www.pdsa.org.uk

W: www.ford-and-etal.co.uk/heathershaw-mill T: 01890 820488

E: miller@heathershawmill.org.uk

W: www.holyislandcrown.co.uk   E: crownandanchor@gmx.com

W: www.holy-island.info/lhc/shop   E: lindisfarne-centre@uk2.net

Printed and Published by

Quacks the Printer,

7 Grape lane,

Petergate,

York YO1 7HU

t 01904 635967 www.radiusonline.info

Whether you visit the island for a few hours or stay for several weeks the aim of this book is to help capture some of the memories.

Stepping onto the island is stepping back in time and provides an escape from the pressures of modern life. Holy Island is an extraordinary place, it can be whatever you want it to be, with its unique history, character and atmosphere enhanced by the sea's ever-changing presence.

Its people, its food and tranquility are hopefully captured here in some small way. The sound of traffic is replaced by the rhythm of the waves lapping at the shore, the cacophony of bird song and the haunting sound of seals on the sandbanks. However, you have spent your time - walking, relaxing (whatever the weather, from sun to snow) this book will hopefully bring back memories of a beautiful place visited and wonderful food eaten.

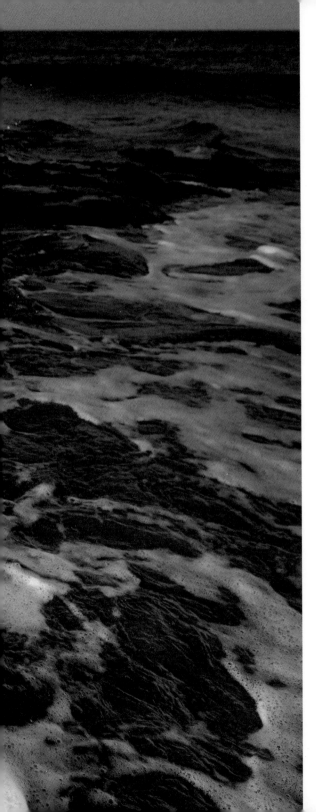

Contents

Foreword

Harry Gration

(Television presenter and Author)

Go into any book shop and you are overwhelmed by the casserole of cook books from around the globe, but many fail to give a real insight into a region or country. What I love about Victoria's and Roy's creation is that it is much more than just a list of recipes.

Here is a snap shot of life on Holy Island with magical creations sweet and warming, few of us would dare to resist.

The photos are stunning and intermingled with unique and special local dishes, many passed down through generations of Victoria's family, and stories of an island steeped in history. The book provides the perfect memory of your trip to one of the greatest places on earth!

So, what more could you wish for in a keepsake for the coffee table, or to be covered in flour in the kitchen . Great food, for all seasons and occasions, a very special history and the occasional surprise.

For me this book ticks so many boxes for birthdays, Christmas or people like me who couldn't cook an egg! Now I have no excuse. It's worth telling your friends about.

Roy's Story

When I was a kid, every weekend meant a family visit to the coast. My mum, grandma, Snoopy the old English sheepdog, and I would squeeze into a 1966 Mini Cooper and set off from Hammersmith down the A3 to Worthing, armed with just a football, swimming trunks, a Kodak instamatic and, if truly blessed, three Danish pastries. Nothing more.

Meanwhile, our friends and neighbour, who used to join us on the beach seemed to take ages to unload their car. It was packed with food and provisions, deck-chairs and general beach paraphernalia. While I watched on enviously, sitting amongst the seaweed and stones, they'd work their way through prawn cocktails, salads, cheese and chutneys, homemade jam and freshly baked chocolate cake. Having feasted, they'd wash it all down with a glass of wine and home-brewed beer, followed by hot tea from a flask.

Yet despite our lack of luxuries, my love for the coast and homemade food was only heightened. Those wonderful memories of simple pleasures: taking my first pictures, paddling, walking, lazing, followed by a two hour drive home squashed next to either grandma or a rather large, wet, hairy dog, will never fade.

In the winter of 2000 I eventually made the trip to Holy Island with my own family and dogs. And yes, the car was full of good food. I delighted in sharing my nostalgic reminisces with my young son. I like to think my mother, who was sitting with him, just as my grandmother had with me, was smiling too.

I don't think anything can quite prepare you for the first sight of Lindisfarne and its approach. Driving down the causeway so close to the water's edge, feeling slightly apprehensive about the gusting sand, the emergency huts protruding like beacons out of the foggy gloom and the mysterious poles reaching out of the sea, all served to captivate us.

Only later did we discover that the poles marked the route of the Pilgrims' Way and were there as a guide and memorial to the journeys, both past and present.

During that holiday we walked on deserted beaches - one moment in glorious sunshine, another in hailstones. Whatever the weather, it was impossible not to feel uplifted, for Holy Island provided an escape from reality and the frantic pace of life.

Exhausted dogs, a child with rosy cheeks, a wonderful cosy cottage in the heart of the village, a log burner glowing at dusk, a glass of mead or whiskey, a visit to one of the local pubs for local ale and fresh food. I also discovered that the island was one of the best places to take photographs - the changing light, the landscapes, the history - what more could anyone want?

This picture is from a gathering of the *Old Grey Whistle Test* family. The iconic television programme had run for many years on BBC2. It was the first time they had been together for nearly 30 years. The occasion was my mother's 80th birthday. The environment I grew up in had a huge influence on my career path. From the age of six I would sit at the back of the gallery, listening to the music, the director, and production assistant as they did their work, watching the cameramen frame shots and seeing the artists perform. There was no career for me other than becoming a television director. And I will always thank my mum and these wonderful people captured here for their support and friendship.

Today I might be directing a live programme, sitting in traffic or opening a bank statement and I often find my mind wanders back to those days on the island.

Holy Island is, in all senses, a retreat.

Victoria's Story

I found my love for all things food at a very young age. I come from a family of food obsessives and seem to have inherited the passion for cooking from my parents. As you will see in the book, a lot of my recipes are "borrowed" from family members. My interest began with baking, cakes mainly. It was my grandma who taught me the basics. I can still picture myself as a little girl making my very first scones with her and believe it or not that very same recipe I am sharing with you now.

I found my love for Holy Island much later in life. I met my husband way back in my first job (as I'm sure you can guess) as a waitress. We soon discovered our enthusiasm for the catering industry and each other. Before long we made the huge leap to open our own café.

Pilgrims coffee house was born in 2006 with very little experience or sleep but with an abundance of passion and drive. Our aim has always been to offer honest home made food using the best quality local ingredients and offer a friendly face. We now even roast our own coffee!

The café has been my life since I left school and it's safe to say I have never looked back. Not many people can say they enjoy their job but I live for mine! We have gained a lot in the last 10 years. Not only a great deal of happy memories but a few (or more) grey hairs and a book full of recipes. Working in the café kitchen has allowed me to be creative with food and over time I have picked up a few neat little tricks.

This book contains all of my most successful recipes. The recipes I have chosen are all inspired by the produce available on Holy Island and the surrounding areas of the beautiful North East. Some are family heirlooms, some are old fashioned and some are completely original (code for made up) but all are easy to make and delicious.

Spring

Watching the sailing boats and the fishing boats bobbing about in the still waters of the harbour is always special, whatever the weather. A safe haven for travellers and pilgrims, a naval base in 1543 and 1639 due to the threat of the Scottish and a refuge for five Norwegians escaping mainland Europe in World War 2. A place of industry throughout the centuries but now just six fishing boats work out of the island compared to 36 in the later part of the 19th century.

Causeway Cockles

Once a common sight, locals would have raked for cockles on the causeway. Now a treasured past time the men and women would go out on a low tide with their rake and bucket to bring home a simple supper for the family.

This is a classic potting recipe, an old fashioned method for preserving a variety of meats and seafood.

Ingredients:

350g cooked and shelled cockles

200g salted butter

1 tsp cayenne pepper

½ tsp mace or nutmeg

1 tsp garlic salt

1 lemon zest only

Method: ready in 1 hour 5 minutes

1. Spoon the cockles evenly between 4 ramekins.

2. In a sauce pan, gently melt together the butter, spices and seasonings for 1-2 minutes.

3. Pour the infused melted butter over the cockles.

4. Chill in the fridge to set for 1 hour.

Cook's Notes

Langoustine Burger

'The harrowing inroads of heathen men made lamentable havoc in the church of god in Holy Island, by rapine and slaughter.' The Anglo Saxon chronicle.

793AD began the invasions of the Island by terrifying Viking marauders, devastating the church and its community by means of robbery and slaughter.

This burger is inspired by an old Viking recipe I found, only I am using our local Langoustine and pork instead of the white fish that would have been used.

Ingredients: serves 4

- 360g raw Langoustine tails (large prawns will do just fine)
- 200g pork mince
- 1 tbsp corn flour
- 1 tbsp chopped parsley
- 1/2 juiced lemon
- 1tsp salt and pepper
- Oil for frying

Method: ready in 15 minutes

1. In a food processor blend all the ingredients together to a firm paste.

2. Shape the mixture into 4 equal burgers approximately 2cm thick.

3. In a pan, fry the burgers in hot oil until cooked through for approximately 5 minutes each side.

Cook's Notes

_____

_____

_____

_____

Several years ago I produced a series for Yorkshire Television called *Cooking for Ages*. We learnt a huge amount about dishes that appealed at certain times throughout history. One of the most amazing was peacock and swan. We went to Rievaulx Abbey in North Yorkshire and Richmond Castle where re-enactment groups held weekends celebrating the history of the location and its people. Both the 'monks' and the 'soldiers' created simple, healthy and delicious recipes. These gatherings were very similar to the Viking re-enactment groups that come to Holy Island every summer. One consistent meal throughout history was known as pottage.

Lamb Pottage

Basically this is a thick soup or stew made by boiling vegetables, grains and if the hunting had been good, meat or fish. The key to its success was that everything was thrown into a huge pot over the fire first thing in the morning, and by lunchtime the food was ready to eat.

The beauty of the pottage was that as the pot started to empty at lunch time, more vegetables and other ingredients were thrown in. So by dinner time, a new style of pottage had been created. Wonderful and delicious.

This is an old family recipe passed down the generations. It was always my favourite meal for supper. Don't be put off by its simplicity - the taste is STEWpendous. My mother used to begin preparing this dish a day in advance using a cheap cut (bones and all) however I have simplified the method to save us all precious time.

Ingredients: serves 4

- 500g diced lamb shoulder
- 1l lamb stock
- 2l water
- 250g diced onion
- 250g diced carrot
- 250g diced potatoes
- 150g barley
- 150g finely sliced spring cabbage
- Salt and pepper

Method: ready in 2 hours

1. In a large soup pan, boil the lamb in the stock and water for 1 hour until soft and tender.

2. Stir in the onions, carrots, potatoes and barley to the boiling stock. Continue to boil for 40 minutes until all the ingredients are cooked through.

3. Stir in the cabbage and continue to boil for 5 minutes until just cooked.

4. Season generously.

In 2003, Stan Timmins based a stunning garden design on the famous Lindisfarne Gospels, it won him a silver medal at the Chelsea Flower Show. The garden was transferred to the island and officially opened on the 19th September 2004. It is found close to the Lindisfarne Gospel Museum.

Continuing the walk around the island you come across a true hidden gem. It's close to the castle and appears, at first sight, a small walled garden. But it is far from insignificant. The wooden gate leads to Gertrude Jekyll's treasure.

There has been a garden at this site for centuries. It was first constructed by the troops living at the castle during the Middle Ages and Renaissance, and was used to grow vegetables, and herbs. It is in an ideal location, south facing in order to get as much of the northern sun as possible. In 1911, Edward Hudson decided to restore the garden and he brought in his friend, Gertrude – hence the name.

As time passed, the garden fell into disrepair. But in 2003, the National Trust undertook a restoration programme to return the garden to the original Jekyll design. It is a truly remarkable place, somewhere where you can sit in solitude or with friends or family, and always with people who respect its beauty.

Protected from the wind, the colours and diversity of plants and herbs, vegetables and flowers are almost overwhelming. It is a secret garden and stirs memories of childhood. I used to play hide and seek with my young lad on long summer evenings when the tide had come in and the island returned to a place of tranquility. The dogs used to join in as well, always giving away my hiding place much to my sons delight. Happy days.

Gertrude's Garden Dressing

This is a recipe inspired by Gertrude Jekyll's beautiful flower garden. A garden that would have once provided essential vegetables, herds and spices for the troops living in the castle.

Ingredients: serves 12

- 1 anchovy fillet
- 1/2 garlic clove
- 150g mayonnaise
- 75g sour cream
- 60g parsley
- 30g tarragon
- 30g chives
- 1 tbsp lemon juice
- 1/2 tsp Dijon mustard
- Salt and pepper

Method: ready in 15 minutes

1. In a food processor blend all the ingredients together until smooth.
2. Season to taste.

Walking over the island and driving around the coastline it is hard not to be overwhelmed by the beauty of the castles. They serve as a reminder of a time when the threat of attack from overseas, or even closer to home, was ever present. In 1880, the island's castle was purchased by Edward Hudson who converted it from a coastguard station into a private residence.

Holy Island Archives:

'The fishermen fill the gap between teatime and bedtime making new nets or repairing old ones, or adding to their stock of crab pots – it's a never ending job. One rough sea can sweep away every pot they put out, wrecking weeks of labour and putting them out of work for weeks.

The women pass their evenings making rag rugs or string shopping bags, crocheting or embroidering, or knitting quickly and tirelessly in an astonishing range of patterns, which they carry in their heads and which have been handed down through the generations. Bedtime is early, perhaps 8 o'clock for fishermen who have to be up by four to finish baiting lines before they put out to sea. It is early to bed too, for those islanders who add to their income by collecting and selling shellfish.'

Walter White, 1859:

'While crossing the herring beach we had a pretty sight in the departure of a number of boats. Evening was coming on, and one after the other they hoisted sail, stood out of the bay, made a tack, and then away to the open sea, perhaps for five and twenty miles.

...we passed the beach where the fishing boats came in and saw the huge vat round which the women stand to clean the herrings.'

Seawater Potatoes

Perfect for the seasons first crop of new potatoes, this is a fantastic, super, simple way to transform the humble spud into a sweet and salty delight. If you can't get easy access to any seawater then sea salted water will do although it's not quite as much fun.

Ingredients: serves 4

- 500g new potatoes
- 3 litres seawater
- Sea salt

Method: ready in 1 hour

1. Preheat the oven to 180C/160C fan.

2. In a large pan boil the potatoes whole for 20-30 minutes (with their skins on) in the seawater until just under cooked.

3. Drain away the water then turn out the potatoes onto a baking tray.

4. Coat with extra sea salt then bake for 30 minutes in the oven until fully cooked.

Cook's Notes

_____

_____

_____

_____

Catriona's Chicken and Leek Pie

You just can't beat good old Northumbrian hospitality. This recipe conjures up happy memories with good friends and good food. OK, so I stole this recipe from a friend but it is just too good not to share. This is a classic one pot chicken and leek pie with a twist of lemon and tarragon. My friend would make this for me (by request) every time we visited before I finally got the recipe to make it for myself.

Ingredients: serves 4

- 1.5kg whole chicken
- 1 finely sliced large leek
- 1 tbsp finely chopped tarragon
- I whole lemon

- 200g crème fraîche
- 350g puff pastry
- 1 beaten egg

Method: ready in 3 hours

1. Preheat the oven to 180C/160C fan.

2. In a 23cm roasting pan, stuff the chicken with the lemon.

3. Roast the chicken in the oven for 1 hour 30 minutes until fully cooked.

4. Allow the chicken to rest for 30 minutes.

5. Remove the lemon from the chicken before stripping the meat from the carcass, setting both aside. Save the juices in the bottom of the pan.

6. In the roasting pan, fry the leeks in the chicken juices for 5 minutes until soft.

7. Stir in the chicken, tarragon, crème fraîche and juice of the roasted lemon. Season to taste, then remove from the heat.

8. Roll out the pastry on a floured surface approximately ½ cm thick to the shape and size of the roasting pan.

9. Transfer the filling to the roasting pan and cover with the pastry lid before glazing with the beaten egg.

10. Bake the pie in the oven for 30 minutes until golden and crispy.

Cook's Notes

_____

_____

_____

_____

_____

Easter time

As you can imagine, Easter for Holy Island is a very special time. It is as though island life stirs from hibernation and springs back into action. Tourists begin to migrate back, bringing with them a renewed sense of vitality. As an Easter tradition each year, hardy Pilgrims trudge barefoot across the sands following the poles that mark the traditional pilgrim's way, carrying the weight of a large wooden cross in honour of this religious festival. There has been a genuine community on the island since 1082 when several Benedictine monks came to rebuild the priory devastated by the Viking attacks. The church was built in the early part of the 12th Century. The posts that stretch across the sea towards the mainland mark the route used in the time of St. Aidan and Cuthbert and the posts as we now see them were laid out in 1800 to aid the new pilgrims.

Hot Cross Buns

In this recipe, I'rn flavouring the buns with Earl Grey Tea. This blend of tea was named after the Earl Grey of Howick, Northumberland, and was designed to compliment the water found at Howick. A Chinese mandarin set to work in order to create the tea for Charles, the second Earl Grey. As the years passed, Earl Grey Tea became popular and was sold worldwide. But the family had failed to register the trademark and subsequently received no money from the sales.

Ingredients: serves 12

for the buns:

- 500g strong white bread flour
- 50g melted unsalted butter
- 1 tsp salt
- 75g caster sugar
- 7g fast action yeast
- 1 egg (beaten)
- 75g sultana
- 75g mixed peal
- 1 orange zest
- 1 lemon zest
- 300g milk (warm)
- 30g loose Earl Grey tea leaves

for the cross:

- 75g plain flour
- 5 tbsp water

for the glaze:

- Apricot jam

Cook's Notes

_____

_____

_____

Method: ready in 3 hours

1. Preheat the oven to 220C/200C fan.
2. Line a large flat tray with grease proof paper.
3. In a small bowl, infuse the tea leaves in the warm milk for at least 3 minutes.
4. Strain the milk to remove the leaves then add the melted butter and beaten egg.
5. In a separate large bowl, mix together the flour, salt, sugar and yeast.
6. Stir in the infused warm milk mixture to form a sticky dough.
7. On a floured surface knead the dough for 5 minutes until smooth.
8. Return the dough to the bowl, cover with a damp cloth, then leave to rise for 1 hour until it doubles in size.
9. Knead in the dried fruit and zest before shaping into 12 equal round buns.
10. Place the buns evenly (allowing space to expand) on your lined tray.
11. Cover with lightly oiled cling film and leave the buns to rise again for a further hour or until they double in size.
12. For the cross, mix together the flour and water to make a paste then pipe over each bun.
13. Bake in the oven for 15 - 20 minutes until risen and browned.
14. When the buns are cooked, brush with hot apricot jam to glaze.

Always on the lookout for places to walk the dogs, places for picnics, and places to experience a little more of this extraordinary region's history, we discovered a captivating and magical place just a short drive from the island.

The Duddo Stones, are located two miles north of Etal, near to Duddo. They are five neolithic sandstone monoliths sitting on top of a hill amid spectacular countryside.

Around 1890, archaeologist Robert Carr discovered and excavated a pit in the centre of the stones. Charcoal and fragments of bone were revealed which gave rise to the theory that the place was once a cremation burial spot.

There is a two-storey hide at Fenham Flats, with views of the whole sweep of coastline from the Lindisfarne Causeway and Holy Island in the north to Guile Point. It is a lovely walk along the rugged shore, as it offers a unique view of the island and the navigation beacons at Ross sands.

The magical sound of all of the different types of birds and the wonderful sight of seeing many of them flying close to the water. It doesn't matter what time of day you visit the flats but there is something special about it as the sun is setting adding a red tinge to the sky and to the stones of the church and beacons across the calm sea.

There is also a hidden WW2 former observatory that the local farmer has turned into a holiday cottage. It is remote, simple, beautifully styled, furnished and with the best of views. Paradise.

Just across the border into Scotland and one can walk on the stunning National Trust land leading towards St. Abbs head. The lighthouse has been there since 1862. It makes for a stunning walk and again another wonderful opportunity for a picnic.

Mire Loch

As part of the walk to St. Abbs Head there is a magical loch. At the turn of the last century this once boggy area was transformed into a place for recreation. A dam was built to form a fresh water loch to be used for angling. Nearby, a nine hole golf course was also constructed and a boat house was built on the loch.

Now all the remains of the golf course is some visible evidence of the old greens and tees, and the once thriving boat house has fallen into disrepair.

Summer

41

Cuthbert Slice

You will not find this Cuthbert slice recipe anywhere else - it is a complete one off and can only be found at Pilgrim's Café on Holy Island. I know this because I made it up. Hehe!

Inspired by the bright colours of the Lindisfarne gospels, this tray bake is one of Pilgrim's Café trademark dishes and has almost achieved cult status among customers and avid bakers alike.

Ingredients: serves 12

- 250ml nut or vegetable oil
- 250g golden syrup
- 100g light brown sugar
- 250g dessicated coconut
- 250g mixed nuts
- 1 zested and juiced lemon

- 1 zested and juiced orange
- 2tsp cinnamon
- 1tsp nutmeg
- 125g raisins
- 125g glacé cherries
- 1 mashed banana
- 1 heaped tbsp caraway seeds
- 500g oats

Method: ready in 45 minutes

1. Preheat the oven to 180C/160C fan.

2. Line a 20cm by 30cm baking tray with greaseproof paper.

3. In a large bowl, mix together all the ingredients thoroughly.

4. Spread evenly into the lined tray.

5. Bake in the oven for 20 - 30 minutes or until golden.

Cook's Notes

_____
_____
_____
_____
_____
_____
_____
_____
_____
_____
_____

Crab Fritters

Another king crustacian of the north sea is the brown crab. A popular northern sandwich filling, so popular in fact you could once even procure one from the kitchen window of a local fisherman's wife, those were the good old days.

Ingredients: serves 4

- 500g cold mashed potato
- 250g white crab meat
- small bunch wild garlic
- 50g grated parmesan
- salt and pepper
- oil for frying

Method: ready in 20 minutes

1. In a food processor blend together the wild garlic and parmesan untill smooth
2. In a large bowl mix together the mashed potato, crab and green paste then season to taste
3. Shape the mixture into 8 equal cakes approx 2cm thick
4. Fry the crab cakes in hot oil until golden and crisp. 5 mins each side

Cook's Notes

_____

_____

_____

(Wha'll Buy My) Caller Herring

This song reminds us how dangerous the work of fishermen was. Indeed it still is. The song is also about how the fishermen's wives sold the herring in Edinburgh.

Chorus
Wha'll buy my caller herrin
They're bonnie fish and halesome farin,
Wha'll buy my caller herrin,
New drawn frae the Forth.

When ye were sleepin on your pillows,
Dream'd ye aught o our puir fellows,
Darkling as they faced the billows,
Aa to fill the woven willows!

O when the creel o herrin passes
Ladies clad in silk and laces,
Gather in their braw pelisses,
Cast their heads and screw their faces.

O neighbour wives now tent my tellin,
When the bonnie fish ye're sellin,
At a word aye be your dealin,
Truth will stand when a' thing's failin.

Wha'll buy my caller herrin,
They're no brought here without brave darin,
Buy my caller herrin,
Ye little ken their worth:

Wha'll buy my caller herrin.
O ye may ca' them vulgar farin
Wives and mithers maist despairin,
Ca' them lives o men.

Written in 1845

46

'Nets lay in heaps, or stretched out 50 or 60 yards... around almost every door lies a heap of floats and lines, and ample sou'westers hang on the walls.

A few men, wearing thick seagoing jackets, and boots up to their hips, take there way down to the beach with a pile of gear on their shoulders.

They will sail ere long for rumour says the herrings are in the offing.'

Walter White, 1859.

Kipper Pâté

The accidental discovery of smoking herring was allegedly only a stones' throw away from Lindisfarne in the small fishing village Seahouses, by a Mr John Woodger in 1843. The story goes that the fish were left for processing one evening in a small room with a smoking fire. Low and behold the next morning the kipper was born. Ever since then it has been a thriving business for the North East, including the famous Craster kipper.

Ingredients: serves 4

- 225g skinned and boned cooked kippers
- 1 spring onion
- 1 lemon zest and juice
- 100g cream cheese
- 1 tsp grated horseradish
- 1 small bunch of parsley
- Salt and pepper to taste

Method: ready in 15 minutes

1. Blend together all the ingredients in a food processor until smooth.

2. Pass through a fine sieve to remove any tiny bones.

3. Season to taste.

4. Chill in the fridge to set.

The Herring houses, close to the harbour's shore, are now mainly holiday homes. Once, a hive of activity as herrings were smoked here.

During the early years of the 19th century, the coast around Lindisfarne was proving treacherous. During that period the shipwreck of vessels, particularly fishing boats and trawlers, totalled a loss of 700 lives in one year alone. So the white pyramid Emmanuel Head was constructed to aid sailors.

The navigation beacons just across the water from the island, on Ross sands and Emmanuel Head, both serve to help sailors navigate safe passage through dangerous waters.

There has been an RNLI presence on Holy Island since 1789. In 1844, the lifeboat station was built on the shore opposite St Cuthberts Island.

It has remained derelict for years, home to many a pigeon, but over the past year it has been restored.

Hopefully, it will become a museum that can pay a fitting tribute to the men and women who have saved so many lives.

Beacon Brauhaus Beer Battered Fish

There is archaeological evidence to suggest that in Tudor times, Holy Island had its first and only brewery. Since then, the residents of Holy Island (admirably so) have worked hard to keep their prolific pub culture very much alive. Yet no new brewery had ever emerged... until now. The founders of Pilgrims Café and their very own German brewmaster have collaborated to introduce "Beacon Brauhaus" a modern artisan brewery, concocting individually crafted beers for your drinking delight. Also great to cook with, this recipe uses the 'loss of signal' for an unbeatable beer batter, however the 'nightcrawler porter' also makes a very interesting alternative.

Ingredients: serves 4

- 125g plain flour
- 1 tsp baking powder
- 1/2 tsp salt
- 230ml Beacon Brauhaus beer
- 4 white fish fillets (smoked fish is equally amazing)
- Oil for deep frying

Method: ready in 35 minutes

1. Preheat oil in a deep fat fryer to 180C.
2. In a large bowl, mix together the flour, baking powder, salt and beer to a smooth batter.
3. Coat the fish in the batter.
4. Fry the fish in the hot oil for approximately 5 minutes until crisp and golden.

Jerusalem Artichoke Soup

Among other things, Holy Island is most famous for its strong historical connection to the Christian faith. Once home to the mother church to all of Northumbria and to famous Celtic saints such as St Aiden (founder of the Lindisfarne priory) and of course St Cuthbert. Even now it still serves as a spiritual sanctuary to many religious communities from all over the world.

Ingredients: serves 4

- 75g butter
- 50g chopped leeks
- 50g chopped celery
- 125g peeled and chopped onion
- 600g peeled and chopped Jerusalem artichoke
- 1.25 litre stock
- 150ml double cream
- Salt and white pepper

Method: ready in 45 minutes

1. In a large soup pan on a medium heat, sweat the vegetables in the butter (stirring occasionally to stop them from browning) for approximatley 10 minutes.

2. Pour in the stock and simmer for 20 minutes until all the vegetables are well cooked.

3. Blend in a food processor until smooth before adding the double cream - season to taste.

Fruit Scones

Skon or scowne? Well if you're 'up north pet' its skon, so be sure not to get them confused.

Without doubt, these are Pilgrim's Café's number one bestseller (apart from coffee of course). Baked fresh every morning, but you've got to be quick, 'once they're scone, they're scone!'

Ingredients: serves 8

- 375g self raising flour
- 75g softened unsalted butter
- 60g caster sugar
- 450ml milk

- 100g sultanas
- ½ tsp baking powder
- 25g icing sugar

Cook's Notes

_____
_____
_____
_____

Method: ready in 30 minutes

1. Preheat the oven to 220C/200C fan.

2. Line a large flat tray with greaseproof paper.

3. In a large bowl rub together the flour, baking powder and butter to resemble fine breadcrumbs.

4. Stir in the sugar and sultanas.

5. Pour in the milk slowly while continuing to mix until a soft dough is formed.

6. On a floured surface, roll out the dough to 3cm thick.

7. With a 6cm cutter, cut out 8 scones. Reshape when needed.

8. Place the scones on the lined tray before dusting with icing sugar.

9. Bake for 10-15 minutes until risen and golden.

Holy Island Archives

In 1906 James Braid was commissioned to lay out a nine hole golf course in the dunes.

To hopefully bring visitors and their money to the island.

He explained that, '*the new course is one of the wildest and most natural to be found anywhere. It will furnish fine golf that will gladden the hearts of the players of the heroic school. On Holy Island the making of bunkers is a business of the utmost simplicity. You just remove the top turf and the wind does the rest, scooping out the sand and shaping the bunkers in the proper way, proving once again how, golf, of all games, is the most akin to nature.*'

Berwickshire News and General Advertiser, Tuesday 11th 1906.

'*On the 11th June 1907, a golf course was officially opened by Mr and Mrs Crossman. Two cups were presented on the first day's play. Most of the players were guests of Edward Hudson of Lindisfarne Castle. The only requisite not supplied is a pavilion.*'

Berwick Advertiser, 1908.

But, as with the fishing industry, times change and the golf course did not succeed.

Ironically, for the million tourists a year that visit the island '*the course now is barely recognizable and many visitors are unaware of it ever having existed amongst the dunes at the end of the straight lonen.*'

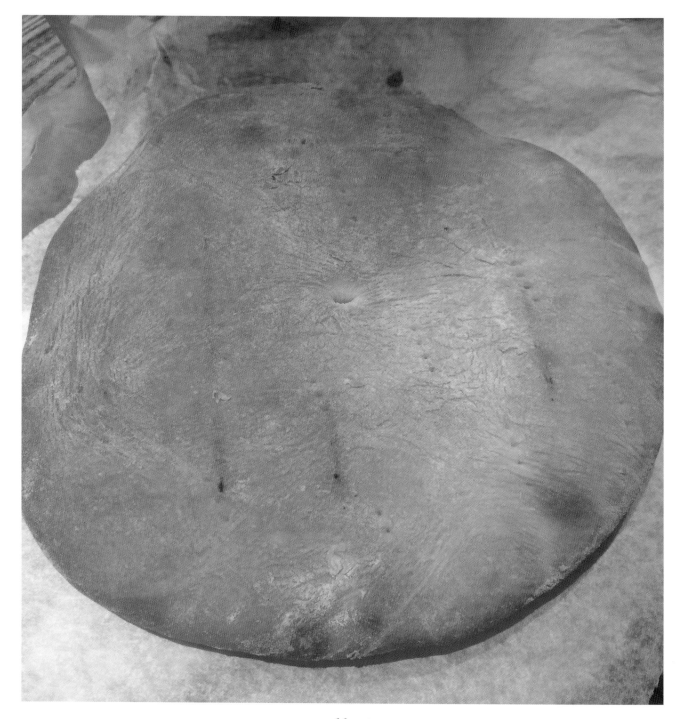

Stottie Cake

A stottie is a type of bread originating in the North East England. It is a flat, round loaf with a hole in the middle made by the baker. The heavy texture of the bread gives the stottie its name. To 'stott' is geordie slang for 'bounce'.

Ingredients: makes 2

- 520g strong plain white flour
- 2tsp salt
- 90g butter
- 7g dried yeast
- 1tsp sugar

- 30ml warm water
- 100ml warm water
- 150ml warm milk

Method: ready in 3 hours

1. Preheat the oven to 220C/200C fan.

2. In a small bowl, mix together the yeast, sugar and 30ml of warm water. Wait until it is frothing then mix in the rest of the hot water and warm milk.

3. In a separate large bowl, rub together the butter, flour and salt to a fine crumb then mix in the liquid until a dough is formed.

4. On a floured surface, knead the dough until smooth and elastic, then return to the bowl to prove (cover with a damp cloth) for 1 hour until doubled in size.

5. Roll into 2 large flat discs about 1inch thick then make a hole in the middle with your finger. Place onto the lined tray before proving again for 30 minutes until doubled in size.

6. Bake for 15 minutes (do not open the oven door) After 15 minutes, quickly turn the bread over then bake for another 5 minutes.

Lemon Drizzle Cake

Sweet, sour and superbly moist! So easy to make and never disappoints. This is probably why it has been on the menu here at pilgrims since day one. A humble cake but boy is it tasty.

Ingredients: serves 12

- 350g butter
- 350g caster sugar
- 350g self raising flour (sifted)

- 6 eggs
- 4 large lemons (zested and juiced)
- 500g icing sugar (sifted)

Method: ready in 1 hour

1. Preheat an oven to 180C/160C fan.

2. Line a baking tray with grease proof paper.

3. In a bowl, cream together the butter and sugar until light and fluffy.

4. Mix in the flour, sugar and lemon zest to a thick batter.

5. Spread the cake mixture evenly into your lined tray.

6. Bake for 25-30 minutes until risen and golden.

7. When the cake is cooked and still hot, pierce the surface all over with a skewer.

8. In another bowl whisk the lemon juice and icing sugar together until smooth and glossy.

9. Pour the lemon icing over the cake slowly and evenly.

The monks were the first to establish the oyster beds and they were believed to be founded in 1381. In 1881, the land belonged to Lord Tankerville. He employed Thomas Bowey to manage the rediscovered beds. Later, in 1953, John Sutherland started farming at Ross, and then found the Island's old beds in 1989 and started farming with his wife Heather.

Oyster Martini

Looking out over the ocean on top of Holy Islands 'heugh' (Northumbrian for hill) you can see Lindisfarne Oyster Farm. Salty and sweet from the rich waters of the North Sea these oysters are a real treat. Here is a slightly more unusual way of serving oysters but be aware this cocktail is not for the faint hearted and can be an acquired taste.

Ingredients: serves 1

- 1 shucked oyster
- 60ml vodka
- 15ml vermouth
- Ice

Method: ready in 5 minutes

1. Place the whole oyster in the bottom of a martini glass.

2. In a cocktail shaker, measure out the spirits then fill with ice.

3. Shake or stir.

4. Slowly strain into the martini glass over the oyster.

Cook's Notes

_____

_____

_____

_____

_____

_____

Lindisfarne Mead Martini

An ancient recipe from a time long ago and famously drank by the monks of the priory. A fortified wine, made from honey known as "the nectar of the gods" this world-renowned tipple is still being made here on Holy Island to this day. This cocktail is light and refreshing, a perfect way to enjoy a historic drink in the modern day.

Ingredients

- 60ml Gin
- 30ml mead
- Ice
- 1cm cube of honeycomb

Method: ready in 5 minutes

1. Place the honeycomb into the bottom of a martini glass.
2. Measure the spirits into a cocktail shaker then fill with ice.
3. Stir until ice cold.
4. Strain over the honey into the martini glass.

Spritzer

Ingredients: serves 1

- 90ml Lindisfarne Mead
- 1 Wedge of Lemon
- 1 Sprig of Lemon Thyme
- Soda Water
- Ice

Method: ready in 5 minutes

1. Muddle the lemon and thyme in the bottom of a glass.
2. Fill with ice.
3. Pour in the mead.
4. Top up with the soda water.

Summer time, walks on the beaches with the children and the dogs, and a wonderful time to take picnics and sit in the dunes. There can be fewer better coastlines to savour the joys of an English summer.

It doesn't matter what time of year I visit the island but it has to be said that there is something rather special about the summer sun and long days walking the dogs and paddling in the 'warm' north sea. I am often captivated by the boats that go out to sea and race back to drop off their catches, which are then rushed off to restaurants around the world.

It's a wonderful sight watching the dancing, diamond waves but for a man who gets seasick in a swimming pool that romance is quickly dispersed when the wind picks up and the white capped waves stretch up and crash over the decks.

Elfreda's Column in the Archives reflects on her visits to Ross Sands, a stones throw from the Island.

'Picnics over there were very enjoyable. One of the fishing boats took us across. The bathing was very safe. After tea the elder people sat down to chat and the younger people explored and walked around the island'

Before the advent of the motor car the doctor from Belford used to come on horseback, stable his horse at the warden's cottage and go down to the shore to be ferried across to the island by boat.'

Victoria's Sponge

A perfect cake for a perfect picnic!

If you're new to baking then this is a great way to start. This is the first cake I ever baked (all those years ago) and I'm still making it the same way today. A lovely summer's treat is a punnet of fresh strawberries grown in the strawberry fields of Holy Island on Coombs Farm. They make the most wonderful strawberry jam, which is just perfect for this cake

Ingredients: serves 12

- 350g soft butter or margarine
- 350g caster sugar
- 350g self raising flour (sifted)
- 6 eggs
- 3 tbsp whole milk
- 2 tsp baking powder
- 1 vanilla pod
- Icing sugar (for dusting the finished sponge)

Filling:

- Double cream (whipped)
- Strawberry Jam

Method: ready in 1 hour 30 minutes

1. Preheat the oven to 180C/160C fan.

2. Line two 20cm by 30cm trays with greaseproof paper.

3. In a large bowl cream the butter and sugar together until light and fluffy.

4. Mix in the flour, eggs, baking powder, milk and vanilla seeds to a thick batter.

6. Spread the mixture evenly into the lined tray.

7. Bake in the oven for 15-20 minutes until risen and golden.

8. Allow to fully cool.

9. Sandwich the jam and whipped cream between the two sponges.

10. Dust the top of the cake with icing sugar.

Cook's Notes

_____

_____

_____

Samphire Soup

If you fancy a bit of foraging along the coastline one sea crop you can always find is seaweed. Samphire is more commonly found along the south coast but look in the right places and you can take home a super tasty super food for absolutely nothing.

Ingredients: Serves 4

- 1 chopped celery stick
- 1 sliced leek
- 1 sliced garlic clove
- 1 tbsp oil
- 1l vegetable stock
- 1 large diced potato
- 350g peas
- 150g samphire
- Salt and pepper
- Oil for frying

Method: ready in 1 hour

1. In a large soup pan, fry the celery, leeks and garlic in hot oil for 5 minutes until soft.

2. Add the stock and potatoes then boil for 20 minutes until just cooked.

3. Stir in the peas and samphire then continue to boil for a further 5 minutes until the vegetables are cooked.

4. In a food processor blend until smooth.

5. Season to taste.

Dr. George Johnstone was born just a few miles from the island in a village near Coldstream in 1797, and he wrote about the island in 1854:

'...men and women were sitting in the sun at the doors, occupied in baiting the lines for the morrow. A number of skates were laid on the tiled roofs of many of the houses, to be dried by the sun, when fully dried they became a favourite relish to the fishermen when drinking their ale.'

Walter White was an American visitor to these shores and wrote a book which, at the time of writing this, is available for download. Northumberland And The Borders, was printed in the second half of the 19th century.

'...we passed the beach where the fishing boats came in and saw the huge vat round which the women stand to clean the herrings.'

Shipwrecks

Walking along the coastline it is possible to see the remains of wrecks buried in the sands. There is something compelling about looking at the old bits of decaying wood and metal. You cannot help but imagine the voyages that the boat must have undertaken and the lives of the people that worked on her.

There have been many wrecks on and around the island. One of the most well known was a steamboat that went ashore in 1915. The Cydonia was loaded with coal and general cargo and a large storm smashed her to pieces on the rocks.

'I remember going out to Sandham Bay and the coal was about twenty feet deep and all along the shore. Carts and horses were carting it home to their houses by the ton. The people said God had sent the ship to tide them over the war.'

A Fisherman's tale

Longstone Island is most famous for its lighthouse and for the legendary tale of Grace Darling. Built in 1825 the lighthouse was made famous by Grace and her father, William. In 1838 on September 7th they rescued 9 survivors from the steamship Forfarshire that had grounded on rocks at Big Harcar. They looked after the stranded victims in the Lighthouse for two days until the vicious storm had passed. All hands would most likely have perished if it had not been for the bravery of Grace Darling and her father. They rowed for nearly a mile across heavy seas to reach the wreck.

There is now a Museum dedicated to the story of Grace Darling in the nearby Village of Bamburgh. The lighthouse was manned until as recently as 1990 and is open to the public between April and October where visitors can see the tiny bedroom from where Grace saw the sailors clinging to the rocks.

Grace's memorial is sited in St. Aidan's church in Bamburgh and is positioned so that it can be seen by passing ships.

A lifeboat in her name was given to Holy Island and she received donations of over £700 including £50 from Queen Victoria.

Grace, along with William, received the silver medal for bravery. The church where she is buried dates from 635AD and Bede died here in 652AD.

The Farne Islands lie between two and three miles off the Northumberland Coast between Seahouses and Bamburgh they are well known for the thousands of breeding puffins that inhabit them in summer. They are also home to one of the most important grey seal colonies in Europe, and their pups (born from late October) and which can be seen here during winter months.

Boat trips leave from Seahouses, sailing around the islands to view the colonies from several vantage points. Seahouses is about 20 miles from the island, between the beautiful villages of Beadnell and Bamburgh.(it is well worth taking the coastal route and stopping off at many of the bays and beaches along the way) This holiday town and fishing port did not exist until 1889 when the harbour was built in order to improve the local fishing and lime industries. Seahouses is known to many as 'The Gateway to the Farne Islands'.

There are between 15 and 28 islands here depending on the tide at the time of a visit.

My son had many happy days playing with friends on the island. They would go looking for crabs off the harbour wall. As they grew older they would go out on the fishing boats and bring home fresh mackerel and lobster, but the reality of the job is much different from that experienced by an adventurous young child.

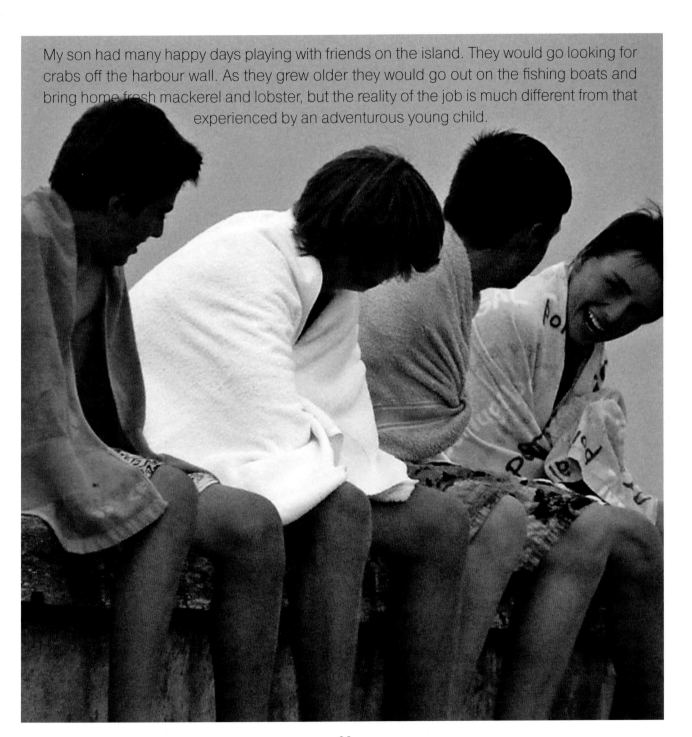

Autumn

St Cuthbert's island with its beach a stones throw from the main island of Lindisfarne has an interesting history. It was the home of St Cuthbert in 678AD after he retired following 12 years in the post of Prior at Lindisfarne Priory. He died here in 687AD, and the church was constructed in his memory in 1370AD.

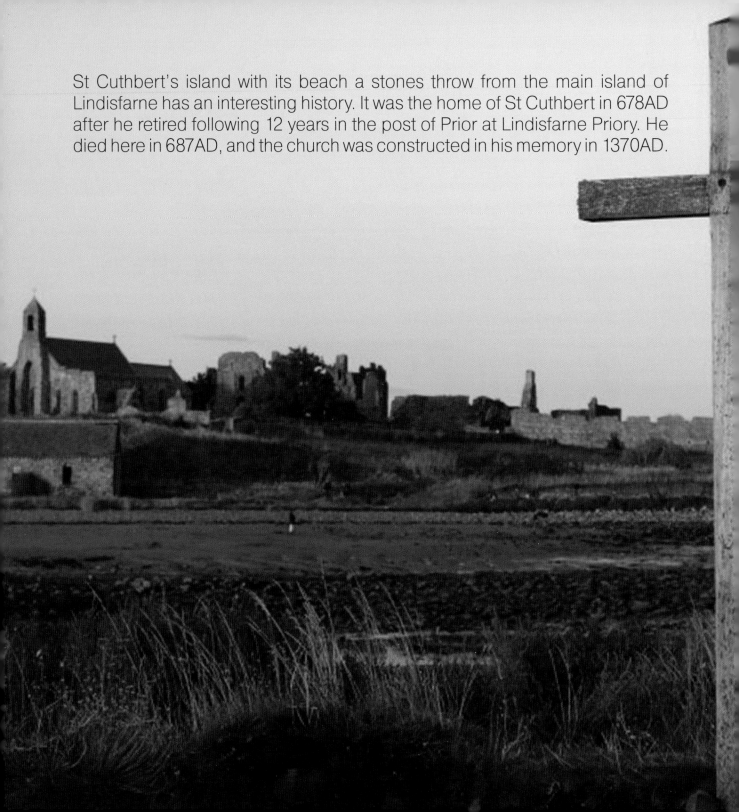

St Cuthbert is said to be the first person to protect birds, even allowing Eider ducks to nest on the steps of his altar! Lindisfarne and the surrounding area is now home to thousands of nesting birds in summer including the Puffin, Cormorants and four types of Tern.

Market day on the island used to be a Saturday. The site of the market cross has been the same since 1826. It is still a focal point and a place where people gather together to watch the birds of prey exhibitions during the summer and sit to eat ice creams.

'In my early years, when I was on holiday at the end of August, the Saturday nearest to St. Aidan's day, August 31st, was regarded as a feast day and travelling people would come with their caravans.

Young people would be given rides and once the day's work had been done the celebrations would go on late into the night.'

Elfreda writing in the 1930's.

To the south of the harbour is a mussel bed where you can often see a lone figure walking the rocks collecting these ingredients for one of our recipes.

Holy Island Archives

'...women are often out before dawn to get to the best mussels and winkle beds and the early sun puts little warmth into fingers raw and numbed by wind and salt water as they tear shells from the rocks.'

Mead Mussels

Being on an island we are very lucky to get access to some wonderful wild produce. Surrounding the island is an abundance of natural mussel beds that cling to the rocky shores. There is no better time to harvest mussels than in the chilly autumn months as they are at their most succulent and plentiful.

This is a classic marinere recipe with a twist, I am using mead instead of white wine.

Ingredients: serves 4
- 1kg washed live mussels
- 3 cloves finely sliced garlic
- 2 finely diced shallots
- 25g salted butter
- 100ml mead
- 100ml double cream
- 1 chopped handful of parsley
- salt and pepper

Method: ready in 15 minutes

1. In a large pan fry the garlic and shallots in hot butter for 5 minutes until soft.

2. Pour in the mead and mussels, cover the pan with a lid then steam for 3-5 minutes until the mussels have opened.

3. Stir in the cream and parsley.

4. Season to taste.

Scottish Shortbread

Being so close to the border, it is only right that we make our own shortbread. This buttery and crunchy biscuit is wonderful on its own but when better with a cup of 'Bari tea'. A local tea from the historic town of Alnwick.

Ingredients: serves 8

- 125g salted butter
- 60g caster sugar
- 125g sifted plain flour
- 60g sifted corn flour

Method: ready in 1 hour

1. Preheat the oven to 190C/170C fan.

2. Line a tray with grease proof paper.

3. In a large bowl cream together the butter and sugar until light and fluffy.

4. Mix in the plain and corn flour to a crumbly dough.

5. On a floured surface lightly knead to a soft dough.

6. Roll out a 1cm thick circle. Cut the circle into 8 equal segments.

7. Place onto the lined tray (slightly separate the segments) then chill in the fridge for 30 minutes.

8. Bake in the oven for 20 minutes until the biscuits are lightly golden.

On the last part of the walk to the Crown and Anchor Inn from our cottage, you go through turnstiles. They have been seen here since the late 18th century. It is thought turnstiles were built rather than a gate so that fishermen, carrying their gear, didn't have to put it down but could just push their way through.

Ham Hock and Pease Pudding Soup

Every fishing community has their own eccentricities and superstitions. For as long as I have known, it has been a great taboo on Holy Island to mention the animal P.I.G. as they are thought to bring bad luck out at sea.

This soup has all the best flavours of the typically northern dish, ham and pease pudding, best served with a big wedge of stottie.

Ingredients: serves 6

- 2kg ham hock
- 5l water
- 2 bay leaves
- 3 cloves garlic
- 5 black peppercorns
- 2 peeled and chopped onions
- 3 chopped carrots
- 2 chopped celery sticks
- 500g yellow split peas
- 1 tbsp English mustard

Method: ready in 3 hours 30 minutes

1. In a large soup pan boil the hock in the water for 2 hours with the bay, garlic, pepper, onion, carrot and celery until the ham begins to fall apart.

2. Remove the hock from the stock and set aside.

3. Add the split peas to the boiling stock then simmer for 1 hour until the lentils are cooked.

4. Remove the bay leaves, then in a food processor blend until smooth.

5. Strip the meat from the bone into bite sized shreds then stir into the soup along with English mustard.

Cook's Notes

_____
_____
_____
_____
_____
_____
_____

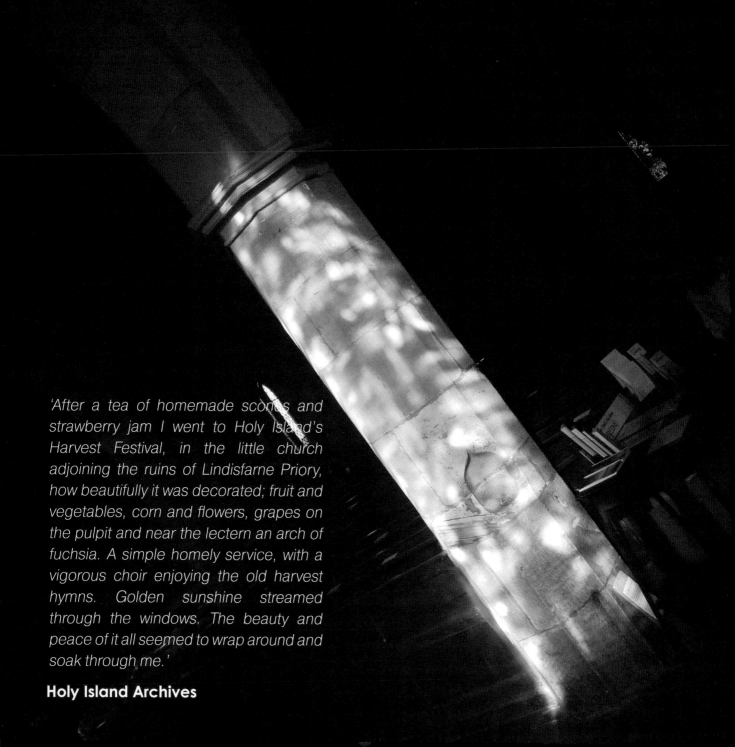

'After a tea of homemade scones and strawberry jam I went to Holy Island's Harvest Festival, in the little church adjoining the ruins of Lindisfarne Priory, how beautifully it was decorated; fruit and vegetables, corn and flowers, grapes on the pulpit and near the lectern an arch of fuchsia. A simple homely service, with a vigorous choir enjoying the old harvest hymns. Golden sunshine streamed through the windows. The beauty and peace of it all seemed to wrap around and soak through me.'

Holy Island Archives

Holy Island Archives

'The vicar was ill and the schoolmaster took the service. As he prayed for the men of the island now serving on land, in the air, and on the sea I thought of the horror of war. But a peacefulness came upon me as I thought of the tranquility of the island and when the monks lived here and how beautiful on this sunny day in wartime was the island called holy.'

For much of the Middle Ages, Belford was at the forefront of the ongoing border conflict between the Scots and the English.

In 1272 it is recorded that Walter de Huntercombe, the Lord of the Manor, was charged with 'assisting pirates'! They had seized, by force, goods belonging to some wealthy Spanish merchants and landed with their booty on Holy Island.

In nearby Etal is Heathershaw Mill where some of the flour used in our cakes comes from. On the banks of the River Till, this is the only working water mill in Northumberland. Powered by a sixteen foot water wheel, there is a history of over 700 years of milling on this site. In around 1830, the mill was enlarged to its present form, servicing a large area including local farm labourers who received all or part of their wages in corn. But rural population declined, and by 1909, the mill was unused. As time passed, the mill became derelict, flooded and filled with silt, and seemed destined for demolition.

However, in 1972 Eric Griffiths formed the Heathershaw Mill Charitable Trust in order to restore the mill and create a working museum. The silt and debris were dug out by hand, the millstones and water mill renovated and the gearwheels and shafts repaired. The mill reopened in May 1975.

113

Cheese Scones

We all have our (top secret) family recipes. It was my mother who taught me to bake and who shared all her secrets with me. One of her specialties were scones, cheese scones in particular. We both use the same family recipe only, much to her dismay, I have tweaked mine slightly. It has now become a regular cause for debate among the family as to who really makes the best cheese scones.

Ingredients: serves 8

- 375g self raising flour
- 75g softened butter
- 150g grated cheddar cheese
- ½ tsp salt

- ½ tsp baking powder
- 1tsp honey mustard
- Approximately 400ml milk
- 1 egg

Method: ready in 30 minutes

1. Preheat the oven to 220C/200 fan.

2. Line a tray with greaseproof paper.

3. In a large bowl, rub together the flour, baking powder and butter to resemble breadcrumbs.

4. Stir in the salt, cheese and honey mustard.

5. Pour in the milk slowly while continuously mixing until a soft dough is formed.

6. On a floured surface roll out the dough about 3cm thick.

7. With a 6cm cutter cut out 8 scones, reshaping when needed.

8. Place on the lined tray then glaze with the beaten egg.

9. Bake for approximately 15 minutes until risen and golden.

Pheasant Cassoulet

It has been a time-honoured tradition for the Holy Island shoot to host an annual supper. At the end of the wildfowling season, game birds are still roasted with all the trimmings in celebration of a bountiful harvest.

My dad is a keen shot, so we often have pheasant overflowing in our freezers. Consequently, I have cooked this bird in many different ways but this recipe is the way I enjoy it most.

Ingredients: serves 4

- The breasts and legs of 1 pheasant
- 3 tbsp plain flour
- 250g bacon lardons
- 1 diced celery stick
- 1 peeled and diced onion
- 1 diced carrot
- 6 whole cloves garlic
- 1 drained tin haricot beans
- 125ml white wine
- 250ml chicken stock
- 1 small bunch thyme
- 1 tbsp olive oil

Method: ready in 1 hour

1. Preheat the oven to 180C/160C fan.

2. Coat the pheasant in the flour.

3. In a large casserole pan, fry the pheasant and bacon in hot oil with the celery, onion, carrot, garlic and thyme until the meat and vegetables caramelise.

4. Deglaze the pan with the white wine.

5. Stir in the beans and stock.

6. Bake in the oven for 30 minutes until golden on top.

Carrot Cake

People often ask me how I manage to resist all the Café's lovely cakes. The truth is I don't and this one is my biggest weakness.

At one time Holy Island would have grown all of its own fruit and vegetables, so what better way to use the humble carrot than this?

Ingredients : serves 12
Cake:

- 650g grated carrots

- 500g soft brown sugar

- 170g sultanas

- 4 eggs

- 250ml vegetable oil

- 2 tsps vanilla extract

- 250g drained crushed pineapple

- 375g plain flour

- 1 1/2 tsp bicarbonate of soda

- 1 tsp salt

- 4 tsps ground cinnamon

- 120g chopped walnuts

For the icing:

- 250g softened unsalted butter

- 175g sifted icing sugar

- 250g cream cheese (room temperature)

Method: ready in 1 hour 30 minutes

1. Preheat the oven to 180C/160C fan.

2. Line a 20cm by 30cm tray with greaseproof paper.

3. In a large bowl mix together all the cake ingredients to a thick batter.

4. Pour the mixture into the prepared tray.

5. Bake for 35-40 minutes until risen and browned.

6. Allow the cake to cool.

Icing

7. In another bowl whip together the butter and icing sugar until light and fluffy.

8. Fold in the cream cheese until smooth.

9. Spread over the cooled carrot cake.

Cook's Notes

_____
_____
_____

Pilgrim's Coffee Cake

Of course I can only recommend Pilgrims freshly roasted coffee. If for some unfortunate reason your coffee stocks have ran dry I suppose some other coffee will do!

Ingredients: serves 12

- 250mls espresso
- 250g salted butter
- 50g cocoa powder
- 400g caster sugar
- 150mls sour cream
- 2 eggs
- 1 tbsp vanilla extract
- 300g plain flour
- 200g chopped walnuts
- 2½ tsps bicarbonate of soda

For the icing

- 250g unsalted butter
- 250g sifted icing sugar
- 120mls espresso

Method: ready in 1 hour 30 minutes

1. Preheat the oven to 180C/160C fan.

2. Line a 20cm by 30cm tray with greaseproof paper.

3. In a large bowl whisk together the butter and sugar until light and fluffy.

4. Mix in the espresso, cocoa, sugar, sour cream, eggs, vanilla, flour, bicarbonate of soda and walnuts to a loose batter.

5. Pour the cake mixture into the prepared tray.

6. Bake for 30-40 minutes until risen and dark brown.

7. Allow the cake to cool.

Icing

8. In another bowl whip together the butter and icing sugar until light and fluffy.

9. Fold in the espresso until smooth.

10. Spread over the cooled coffee cake.

121

Espresso Martini

We have been roasting coffee now for over 3 years, we began roasting in a potting shed and have now upgraded to a yurt. We take great care to select only the finest beans of the season and roast them up in order to serve you the freshest coffee this side of the causeway.

If you like coffee, then you will love this cocktail! Satisfyingly strong, with subtle sweetness and oh so velvety smooth.

Ingredients: serves 1

- 30ml vodka
- 20ml kahlua
- 10ml creme de cacoa
- 50ml espresso
- Ice

Method: ready in 5 minutes

1. Measure all the ingredients into a cocktail shaker then fill with ice.
2. Shake until cool and frothy.
3. Strain into a martini glass.

Winter

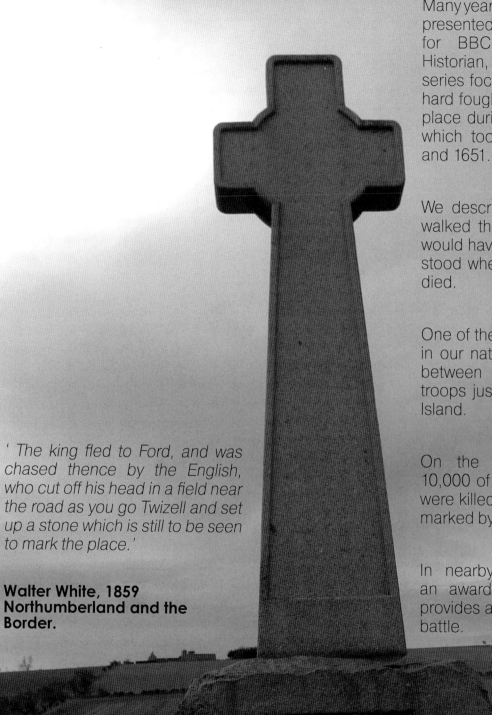

Many years ago I produced and co-presented a series of programmes for BBC Radio with, Military Historian, Dr Peter Newman. The series focused on the bloody and hard fought battles that had taken place during the English Civil War which took place between 1642 and 1651.

We described the scenes as we walked the paths that the troops would have taken to battle and we stood where they had fought and died.

One of the most significant battles in our nation's history took place between Scottish and English troops just a few miles from Holy Island.

On the 9th September 1513, 10,000 of King James IV's troops were killed. The battlefield is today marked by this granite cross.

In nearby Etal Castle there is an award-winning museum that provides a detailed account of the battle.

' The king fled to Ford, and was chased thence by the English, who cut off his head in a field near the road as you go Twizell and set up a stone which is still to be seen to mark the place.'

Walter White, 1859
Northumberland and the
Border.

My visit to the surrounding area and the church brought back memories of the programmes and Peter's words as he graphically described the horrific scenes of battle and the harsh reality of the brutality of hand to hand combat. One of his comments that has always stayed with me is that the dead and wounded were being thrown into pits together and left to rot as one.

The location, the conditions, heavy waterlogged ground, and a weapon, the long pike, that could not be used effectively on the day, meant that in just over two hours around 9,000 Scottish troops, including the King and many of the country's ruling class were dead. It was the final battle of its sort to be fought in the country as small arms started to replace the sword.

Sticky Date Selkirk Bannock

Although the island is always welcoming, whatever the time of year, the archives in the Island's museum make it clear that the winters, can be extremely harsh and challenging. So locally sourced, nutritious and nourishing homemade food has always been essential.

'Bannock' is an old Celtic word for bread. The Selkirk Bannock is a rich fruit loaf named after a town in the Scottish borders from where it was originally made. The first known maker of this variety was a baker named Robbie Douglas, who opened his shop in Selkirk in 1859.

Ingredients: serves 8

- 7g sachet fast-action yeast
- 250ml warm water
- 1 tsp caster sugar
- 250g strong wholemeal flour
- 250g strong white flour
- 125g melted unsalted butter
- 250g chopped dates
- 50g soft brown sugar
- Milk for glazing

Method: ready in 3 hours

1. Preheat the oven to 180C/160C fan.

2. Line a 23cm diameter cake tin with grease proof paper.

3. In a large bowl, mix together the yeast, caster sugar and warm water then let it stand for 10 minutes until the mixture becomes frothy.

4. Stir in the flour and butter to form a dough.

5. On a floured surface knead the dough for 5 minutes until soft and smooth.

6. Return the dough to the bowl then prove for 1 hour until doubled in size.

7. Knead in the dates and brown sugar until evenly distributed.

8. Shape the dough into a round loaf, place into the tin then prove again for 30 minutes until doubled in size.

9. Glaze the bannock with the milk then bake in the oven for 35-40 minutes until risen and browned.

132

In the biting cold winds and sleet just imagine the life of a fisherman. Dressed in leather, seaboots and heavy woollen jumpers with no waterproof properties. A man was quickly soaked to the skin. Add the wind factor as well and it is clear to see just how hard a lifestyle this was and still is to this day.

Holy Island Skink

Inspired by the classic Scottish fish soup 'Cullen Skink'. This humble soup is deliciously rich and full of warming winter ingredients. In old Scottish recipe books you would have used a 'finnan haddie'. A regional cold smoked haddock, but any smoked white fish will do brilliantly.

Ingredients: serves 4

- 25g salted butter
- 100g bacon lardons
- 2 finely sliced leeks
- 3 cloves finely sliced garlic
- 500g peeled diced potatoes

- 1 l chicken stock
- 500ml milk
- 250g diced smoked fish fillet
- 150ml cream
- Salt and pepper

Method: ready in 45 minutes

1. In a large soup pan, fry the bacon, leeks and garlic in hot butter for 5 minutes until soft.

2. Pour in the chicken stock, bring to the boil then add the potatoes. Boil for 20 minutes until cooked.

3. Pour in the milk, reduce to a simmer then add the fish. Simmer for 5 minutes until just cooked through.

4. Stir in the cream then season with the salt and pepper to taste.

Cook's Notes

135

Panhaggerty

A traditional Northumbrian potato dish - the name coming from the old English word 'panhin' meaning small pan. Hearty and rich, it makes great comfort food. This rustic grub is simple to make and with few, basic ingredients it's a real cheap eat, making it a popular meal for northern families throughout history.

Ingredients: serves 4

- 25g salted butter
- 500g thinly sliced potatoes
- 200g thinly sliced onions

- 150g grated cheddar cheese
- Small bunch of thyme leaves
- Garlic salt and pepper

Method: ready in 1 hour

1. Preheat the oven to 180C/160 fan.

2. Grease a 25cm diameter, oven proof frying pan with the butter.

3. Divide each of the other ingredients into three equal portions.

4. Layer the ingredients in the pan; begin with a layer of potatoes (slightly overlapping each slice), then onion, then cheese, seasoning with the salt, pepper and thyme after each layer.

5. Repeat to make 3 layers in total.

6. Bake in the oven for 40-50 minutes until the potatoes are cooked through and the cheesy top is golden and crisp.

Cook's Notes

_____
_____
_____
_____
_____
_____
_____
_____

138

Holy Island Archives

' ... Holy Island is crowded in the summer with visitors who are so fascinated to coming time and time again. Anyone can be a Crusoe for a fortnight, but let me give you a winter scene in a place that is a true island at full tide.

Water is an issue. There are two public pumps. A family needs four buckets a day which means two trips for a member of the family in sunshine or blizzard.

Washing, laundry and toilet are done in rainwater collected in butts.'

David Simpson writing in the 1940s and written in a local journal by his son, Alan.

'Some houses do have boilers behind the fireplace to heat the water. But the majority have to use the 'sma' kettle or the 'muttle' according to whether it is for a pot of tea or a bath in the washbowl.'

The Scottish influence on our recipes is clear to see. This is not due just to the geographical positioning of the island but also the extraordinary history of the region, frequently bloodthirsty in nature and certainly never dull.

Just a few miles away from the Lindisfarne Island is Berwick. Berwick's story over its past 500 years as an outpost of England is connected to the history of its positioning on the wrong bank of the River Tweed. Five bridges dating back to the 1100's have been built across the river.

Walking through the town today it is hard to believe just how important historically this small town on the Tweed has been to the nations of both England and Scotland.

From 1018AD and for a period of about 250 years, Berwick was one of the most important towns and ports in Scotland. But in 1296, Edward I of England sacked the town and slaughtered 8,000 of its residents. This marked the start of two centuries of chaos, during which the town changed hands every 15 years.

Berwick also has a near intact town wall which surrounds it and takes about 45 minutes to walk round. It is home to the Berwick Barracks, built in 1715 following the Jacobite uprising to house a defensive garrison. Berwick is a town whose hidden history is a joy to uncover.

The painter Lowry holidayed in Berwick and 18 of his paintings have been reproduced on information boards around the town.

'A custom prevails in these parts of holding what may be described as a salmon picnic...
The fish are transferred to the kettle and boiled, and sports and pastimes end the holiday'.

Walter White (writing in the 1800's).

Close to the river is an entrance to one of Berwick's Ice Houses built in 1790. Ice brought new riches to the salmon traders. London was a week's sailing away and the fish used to have to be pickled in vinegar or salted. Like this it may fetch 1/2 penny per kilo, whereas the fresh fish packed in ice, a Chinese idea, increased the price to 10 pennies per kilo.

Haggis Scotch Egg

At the risk of upsetting a proud nation, it has been known that the much-loved haggis was once an English recipe named 'hagese'. Whatever the origin of this 'wee beastie' it makes a cracking scotch egg.

Ingredients: serves 4

- 300g haggis
- 200g pork sausage meat
- 1 tbsp English mustard
- 4 eggs
- 50g breadcrumbs
- Oil for frying

Method: ready in 20 minutes

1. Preheat the oil in a deep fat fryer to 180C.

2. In a pan of boiling water, soft boil the eggs for 4 minutes.

3. Allow to cool then peel.

4. In a bowl, mix together the haggis, sausage meat and mustard.

5. Shape the meat around the eggs then coat in the oats.

6. Deep fry for 10 minutes until deep golden brown.

Border Tart

A deliciously sweet and fruity tart from the English / Scottish borders. I've added whiskey and local honey from the border hills (Chainbridge honey) in homage to our Scottish neighbours.

Ingredients: serves 12

- 250g sweet shortcrust pastry
- 60ml whiskey
- 300g mixed dried fruit
- 100g melted unsalted butter

- 200g chopped walnuts
- 100g honey
- 2 eggs
- 1 zested and juiced lemon

Method: ready in 2 hours

1. Preheat the oven to 190C/170C fan.

2. Line a 20cm by 25cm tart tin with greaseproof paper.

3. On a floured surface roll out the pastry 2mm thick, place into the tin then cut away the edges.

4. In a bowl soak the dried fruit in the whiskey for 1 hour until plump.

5. Mix in the melted butter; nuts and honey then finally beat in the egg.

6. Pour the mixture evenly over the pastry.

7. Bake in the oven for 25-30 minutes until golden and crisp.

Cooks Notes

_____
_____
_____
_____
_____
_____
_____
_____
_____
_____
_____
_____

The causeway was built in 1954 and clearly has made the journey to and from the island less precarious. Popping into Berwick and other nearby towns for provisions, or having items delivered, has become rather less of a challenge. Historically for the majority of islanders, it was just too expensive to own a pony and cart. The main transport came from the post cart which visited the island twice a day.

The villagers were dependent upon deliveries from the mainland brought by a butcher and by bakers. Coal, also essential, would be brought across whenever possible, and was just dumped at your front door for you to shovel in.

'Bad weather can upset the routine for three weeks and last year the island was cut off, no food or fuel could be delivered. The islanders were compelled to live like one family, pooling supplies and sharing them equally in order to eat and keep warm.'

Holy Island Archives

Walking around the island now it is hard to imagine that it was once a hive of activity related to industry rather than tourism. There are several remains of coal mines, with the tower of the snook being the shaft of the small mine on the island. Iron ore was also mined in the 17th century and there is evidence of quarrying for lime and kilns where lime would have been processed.

A Dundee firm built lime kilns on Lindisfarne in the 1860s, and lime was burnt on the island until at least the end of the 19th century. The kilns were used to produce quicklime (a chemical compound used for mortar and fertilizer). One in five island men worked in the industry and, at its peak, over 100 men were employed.

The kilns are among the most complex in Northumberland. Horses carried limestone along the Holy Island Waggonway, from a quarry on the north side of the island to the lime kilns. There it was burned with coal transported from Dundee on the east coast of Scotland.

There are still some traces of the jetties from which the coal was imported and the lime exported, close by at the foot of the crags. The remains of the wagon way between the quarries and the kilns can still be clearly seen and helps pave the way for a really lovely walk. Close to the shore the view spans across to the Farne Islands, Bamburgh, and Emmanuel Head in the distance. Seeing herons and cormorants on the rocks drying their wings, and listening to the sounds of so many birds and seals, is just overwhelming. I do the walk every day with the dogs when I am on the island. The atmosphere changes constantly as the colour of the sky and the sea and the shapes of the clouds provide an ever-changing inspiration.

Farmer Jimmy's Scotch Pie

A mutton pie originating in bonny Scotland, this substantially scrumptious pie proved popular as a working man's lunch in the industrial era.

Ingredients: serves 4

Filling;

- 500g lamb mince
- 1 tsp nutmeg
- 5 tbsp lamb stock
- Salt and white pepper

Pastry;

- 100g lard
- 150ml water
- 300g plain flour
- ½ tsp salt
- 1 beaten egg

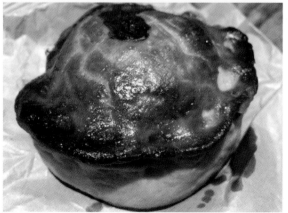

Method: ready in 2 hours

1. Preheat the oven to 200C/180C fan.
2. Line a baking tray with greaseproof paper.

For the filling:

3. In a bowl mix together all the ingredients then divide into four equal balls.

For the pastry:

4. In a saucepan heat the lard, water and salt to boiling point then remove from the heat.
5. Mix in the flour until a dough is formed.
6. On a floured surface, knead the hot dough until smooth.

For the pies:

7. While the dough is still warm cut away ¼ of the pastry for the lids then roll out the remaining dough into 4 x15cm circles, ½ cm thick.

8. Wrap the pastry around the meat leaving enough room to attach a lid. With the remaining dough roll out 4 x 10cm circular lids before attaching to the top of the pie by crimping the edges.

9. Place the pies on the tray before glazing with the beaten egg and piercing a steam hole in the lid.

10. Chill in the fridge to rest for 30 minutes.

11. Bake in the oven for 30-40 minutes until golden and crisp.

Both World Wars had a major impact upon the community on the island. In the aftermath of the First World War, thousands of war memorials were built across Britain. Amongst the most prominent of their designers was the architect Sir Edwin Lutyens, described by Historic England as 'the leading English architect of his generation'. Lutyens designed the Cenotaph on Whitehall in London, which became the focus for the national Remembrance Sunday. Lindisfarne's memorial is one of fifteen war crosses by Lutyens, all sharing a broadly similar design. The memorial is sited on the Heugh, within view of Lutyens's Lindisfarne Castle and its gardens.

The surrounding coast and countryside that can just be seen from the island adds to the magic of both Lindisfarne and Northumberland.

The Cheviots in the near distance lay claim to many wonderful walks and stories. You can spend many hours watching the weather patterns and the spectacular changes in clouds as they roll over the hills.

The area around the island and the Cheviots played an important part in the Second World War.

But, inevitably there was tragedy. In Kirknewton cemetery are the graves of several Canadians killed on a training exercise in the hills.

During the Second World War, it was often the combination of atrocious weather conditions, less advanced navigation systems and simple inexperience that claimed the lives of several Allied airmen – and Germans too – whose planes crashed on the Cheviot and its surrounding hills.

After one crash in particular of a B-17 Flying Fortress with a nine-man American crew aboard, came the now legendary story of rescue by local shepherds including John Dagg and his black and white collie, Sheila. Their heroism was honoured with the award of the Dickin Medal (the animal version of the Victoria Cross) to Sheila. She became the first ever civilian dog to receive the coveted medal with its tri-coloured ribbon. Her master received the British Empire Medal. To date there have been just 68 recipients of the Dickin Medal. As well as dogs, the award had been given to pigeons, horses and a cat.

One remarkable story saw five Norwegians fleeing the Germans in 1941. Their small boat, powered by elbow grease and one engine, ended up landing on the island. They were cautiously welcomed by the islanders who were initially not sure if they were Germans. The five joined the war effort here, learning how to fly Spitfires. In September 2010, a bench and plaque were unveiled at a ceremony in memory of these men.

Corned Beef Hash Pies

Corned beef hash became especially popular in WW2 during rationing. Unfortunately Holy Island did not escape the war. You can still see the evidence today. At the beginning of the causeway stands anti-tank defences that people now use as viewing perches to watch the tide come in.

This is a recipe based on my grandma's famous corned beef pie, only I have given her much-loved creation a new twist of flavour.

Ingredients: serves 4

- 250g shortcrust pastry
- 200g grated potato
- 340g corned beef
- 1 diced onion
- 50g butter
- 6 eggs

Method: ready in 45 minutes

1. Preheat the oven to 190C/170C fan.

2. Line a 20cm by 25cm tray with greaseproof paper.

3. Fry the grated potato, corned beef and onion in hot butter (stirring infrequently) for 20 minutes until well caramelised.

4. On a floured surface, roll out the pastry approx 2mm thick, then place into the prepared tin.

5. Trim the edges then blind bake for 10 minutes until light golden in colour.

6. Fill the cooked pastry case with the corned beef hash mixture.

7. Crack the raw eggs on top to form a lid.

8. Return the pie to the oven and bake for 5 minutes until the eggs are just cooked.

Cook's Notes

_____

_____

_____

_____

_____

_____

Christmas is always a magical time and there can be few better places to celebrate or welcome in the New Year than Holy Island.

Holy Island Archives

'I can remember when no carols were sung until Christmas Eve. We went around the village singing until the New Year. There was something wonderful in being out on a frosty star filled night and hearing carols being sung across the fields and the sea.

We found a good use for holly. I was to climb onto the roof of the house with a good sized piece with a stone tied to it and drop it down the chimney. Obviously the household had been warned of this speedy way of cleaning the chimney. Then after twelfth night the Christmas tree was sometimes used to clean the chimney by dropping it down the chimney. There had to be enough rope on the tree in case it got stuck.'

Chocolate Fudge Brownie (gluten free)

Tablet is a traditional Scottish confection (similar to fudge) dating back to the early 18th century. Having learned her craft from her mother, my sister in law now makes and sells her own scrumptious fudge right next door in THE pilgrims fudge kitchen, how convenient!

Ingredients: serves 12

- 250g unsalted butter
- 375g dark chocolate
- 250g gluten free self raising flour
- 500g caster sugar
- 7 eggs
- 200g chopped pilgrims fudge

Method: ready in 45 minutes

1. Preheat the oven to 180C/160C fan.
2. Line a 20cm by 30cm tray with greaseproof paper.
3. In a large (heat resistant) bowl melt together the butter and chocolate.
4. Mix in the flour, sugar and eggs until smooth and glossy.
5. Spread the brownie mixture evenly into your lined tray.
6. Sprinkle over the pilgrims fudge.
7. Bake for 20-25 minutes until crisp on the outside but gooey in the middle.

Cook's Notes

_____

_____

_____

Mince Pie Martini

Christmas spirit is a welcome warmth in among the bleak and lonely winter months on the island. Festive cheer heats the heart of our community like the log fires in our homes. Not unlike the warmth from this mince pie martini, a glass full of another festive spirit.

Ingredients: serves 1

- 60ml vodka
- 30ml cointreau
- 1 tbsp mincemeat
- 60ml single cream
- Ice

Method: ready in 5 minutes

1. In a cocktail shaker measure out the vodka and mincemeat then fill with ice.

2. Shake with festive joy!

3. Strain into a martini glass.

4. Mix together the cointreau and cream before floating (using the back of a spoon) over the mincemeat infused vodka.

Holy Island Archives:

'As we came out of the church we all chatted together - Mrs. Cromarty and George, Allison and the Bell family and the stranger within the gate. And as I turned the corner and saw the famous 'rainbow' arch of the Priory still standing triumphant against the sky after all these years, and I knew that wars can come and wars can go, but that love and friendship will ever be in the hearts of men and women.'

Holy Island, lindisfarne, Northumberland.
Quite simply an island to savour.

A retreat, an escape for many.

A living, breathing island that embraces
the past whilst looking to the future.

*Nostalgia strips the mind of all but the essence of time. It may be the
waft of a scent, the memory of a favourite food discovered on the island,
the texture of fabric or the simple, clean, pastel shade of a wind charm,
a song on the radio, an old movie or television programme, the sound of
children's laughter in a school playground, or the sound of church bells
in the wind.*

(Hilary Robinson, Author)

Index

I grew up in a small town surrounded by fields and countryside. This provided a glorious place to grow as a kid, it's just a shame, like many other children, I was overly keen for time to pass quickly so I could do much cooler things as a grown-up, pay bills and go to work. If someone said to you, you could spend your days climbing trees, playing tag in a corn field or fishing for sticklebacks in rivers – you'd feel like you've won the lottery, or reached nirvana. To this day the smell of manure takes me floating on a nostalgic trip back to time when the sun always shone and my mum told me to be back when the street lights came on.

(Johnny I 'Anson- radio broadcaster)